Cutting Edge Careers in

MEDICINE

Julie Kosloski

ReferencePoint
Press®

San Diego, CA

About the Author

Julie Kosloski lives in Colorado with her family. She graduated from the University of Northern Colorado with a degree in psychology. After teaching English in Japan for several years, she taught elementary school in Denver. She began working as a freelance proofreader and editor, which led to her interest in writing.

For more information, contact:
ReferencePoint Press, Inc.
PO Box 27779
San Diego, CA 92198
www.ReferencePointPress.com

LIBRARY OF CONGRESS CATALOGING-IN-PUBLICATION DATA

Names: Kosloski, Julie, author.
Title: Cutting edge careers in medicine / by Julie Kosloski.
Description: San Diego, CA : ReferencePoint Press, Inc., 2021. | Series:
  Cutting edge STEM careers | Includes bibliographical references and
  index.
Identifiers: LCCN 2019058575 (print) | LCCN 2019058576 (ebook) | ISBN
  9781682828717 (library binding) | ISBN 9781682828724 (ebook)
Subjects: LCSH: Medicine--Vocational guidance.
Classification: LCC R690 .K67 2021 (print) | LCC R690 (ebook) | DDC
  610.69--dc23
LC record available at https://lccn.loc.gov/2019058575
LC ebook record available at https://lccn.loc.gov/2019058576

Contents

New Frontiers
in Medicine

A woman dressed in white walks down a long, dark corridor. The only light comes from the glow of the machines that surround her. It is quiet except for the steady hum of the equipment. Without all the normal chaos and noise, she can focus on the patients who are attached to these monitors. She is a nocturnist, a medical doctor who practices at night, admitting and treating a wide variety of hospital patients when most of the staff members have gone home. As Dr. Jalila Cunningham says, "A nocturnist is the one that shines in the dark of night when everyone else is fast asleep."[1]

This is just one of the careers in medicine that offer opportunities for the future. The field of medicine is changing dramatically, and there are many ways to become involved in this rewarding field. Teens who study science and math today might go on to pursue a career in research, discovering new ways to prevent and treat illnesses. Or, they could seek a career in a more traditional specialty such as pediatrics or internal medicine. On the other end of the spectrum, brand new medical frontiers are opening up, such as robotic-assisted surgery and three-dimensional printing of replacement organs. Research and advances in technology make this an exciting time to learn more about cutting edge careers in medicine.

Choices, Choices, and More Choices

Medicine is a vast field with three main branches that work together. These branches are clinical careers (doctors and nurses), allied health careers (professionals who collaborate with doctors to provide therapy and treatment), and ancillary careers (those who provide administrative and support services).

Physicians and nurses are likely the first jobs that come to mind when people think of clinical careers. Doctors and nurses are in huge demand, with predicted job growth of more than 14 percent by 2028.

There will be a need for doctors in familiar areas such as family and general medicine. There are also new, fast-growing specialties that are changing the way medicine is practiced. One example is a medical virtualist, also called a telehealth physician, who consults with patients remotely using computers and phones. These doctors treat people living in isolated areas—or consult with doctors to offer second opinions—without requiring long-distance travel by patients. Another emerging field is in cancer immunology. These doctors are seeking ways to help the human immune system fight off malignancies, which will change how cancer is treated.

Nurses are also in demand in traditional fields such as pediatrics and geriatrics, working with patients young and old. But nursing is becoming more specialized, offering fulfilling, cutting edge career options. Some nurses work with specific populations. Nurse-midwives, for instance, provide care in connection with pregnancy, labor, and health after delivery. Neonatal nurses work exclusively with babies in the hospital nursery or neonatal intensive care unit, helping the smallest and most fragile patients.

The second branch of medicine includes people who work together with doctors to provide treatments and therapy. Many of the high-growth jobs are for therapists. This includes physical therapists, who help people improve their movement, and occupational therapists, who help people with disabilities learn to do everyday activities. Other highly sought-after therapists work in the field of mental health. This includes marriage and family counseling, addiction and substance abuse therapy, and nutritional counseling. The focus on preventive medicine and healthy lifestyles has made the allied health field one of great importance and innovation.

Ancillary jobs are the final branch, and they play important roles in the ever-changing world of medicine. Research and innovation cannot be put to practical use without administrative systems and support. There is a need for patient navigators to help patients understand insurance and other aspects of medical

Attributes That Matter to Employers

Written communication skills and the ability to solve problems are at the top of the list of attributes employers look for when considering new hires. This is the finding of a report titled "Job Outlook 2019." The report comes from the National Association of Colleges and Employers (NACE), an organization that surveys employers nationwide to learn more about their hiring plans in connection with recent college graduates. Other desirable attributes include the ability to work in a team setting, showing initiative, analytical skills, and a strong work ethic.

Attribute	% of Respondents
Communication skills (written)	82.0%
Problem-solving skills	80.9%
Ability to work in a team	78.7%
Initiative	74.2%
Analytical/quantitative skills	71.9%
Strong work ethic	70.8%
Communication skills (verbal)	67.4%
Leadership	67.4%
Detail oriented	59.6%
Technical skills	59.6%
Flexibility/adaptability	58.4%
Computer skills	55.1%
Interpersonal skills (relates well to others)	52.8%
Organizational ability	43.8%
Strategic planning skills	38.2%
Tactfulness	25.8%
Creativity	23.6%
Friendly/outgoing personality	22.5%
Entrepreneurial skills/risk-taker	16.9%
Fluency in a foreign language	11.2%

Source: "Job Outlook 2019," NACE, November 2018.
www.odu.edu/content/dam/odu/offices/cmc/docs/nace/2019-nace-job-outlook-survey.pdf.

care. Public health educators are vital to help inform and develop healthier communities and are critical in cases of food poisoning or during an epidemic. Computer and information technologists are essential to the smooth operation of medical offices and hospitals. People who work in informatics—an emerging field that uses data to help improve patient care—are also becoming more important in medicine.

A Promising Future Outlook

The future looks bright for young people who pursue careers in medicine. Many factors contribute to this anticipated growth, such as the aging baby boomer population and longer life expectancy. The entire field of medicine is changing in dynamic ways. One area is personalized medicine, in which doctors treat patients according to their individual characteristics and genetics. This allows doctors to focus on prevention and use the latest research to help people live longer, healthier lives.

Young adults who are interested in any of the vast number of cutting edge STEM careers in medicine should talk to their counselors and teachers about what classes to take and begin planning. Many of today's youth will one day make a difference through a career in medicine, so hard work in science, math, and technology classes will pay off by creating plentiful, rewarding opportunities.

Medical Scientist

What Does a Medical Scientist Do?

Research is the backbone of medicine. Every new medication, vaccine, and treatment is the result of a medical scientist working to improve human health. Medical scientists research diseases and design and conduct studies to prevent and treat them. It can be very rewarding work, as one biomedical scientist comments: "Being able to give those with no hope just a little hope that a new drug might work for them is an amazing feeling."[2]

Medical scientists seek to understand health issues and find cures. They usually do so through a multistage research process. That process involves developing an idea, designing a study, testing in a lab and on humans, collecting and analyzing data, and writing a report. One example would be developing a new drug to slow down a type of cancer. At one point during the process, medical scientists create clinical trials. They work with doctors to find patients who fit the medical criteria and are willing to take part. Medical scientists then run the clinical trials. Usually in such trials, some patients receive the experimental drug and some receive a placebo, which is a substance that looks like medicine but does not have any physical effect. Medical scientists compare the results of the volunteers who take the drug to the results of the volunteers who take the placebo. They monitor all trial participants and collect data. Finally, they analyze the data, draw conclusions about the success of the new drug, and present their results.

Other medical scientists might work on developing products that people take for better health, such as vitamins or various medications. They identify safe drug strengths and work to standardize recommended doses and how a patient takes the drug (for example, by mouth or by an injection). This gives drug companies guidelines to follow for making and distributing medications. Some medical scientists work with biological samples rather than people, studying viruses, bacteria, or infectious agents to understand how they affect people. They can then develop vaccines or drugs to prevent or treat illnesses such as influenza or pneumonia.

Medical scientists often try to understand the causes of disease. For instance, they might want to understand how diet contributes to diabetes or how vaping might lead to lung disease. They might embark on this research with the goal of developing new prevention strategies. Medical scientists who use their research to educate people about health risks, such as the effects of smoking, are called public health scientists. Other medical scientists, called epidemiologists, specialize in tracking health data and deciding how to react when a disease spreads. They track outbreaks of diseases, such as coronavirus, to treat the illnesses and also prevent their spread in the future. They are sometimes called the "disease detectives" of the medical science world.

The Workday

The daily schedule for medical scientists depends on their current stage of research. Typically, they work a regular 9 a.m. to 5 p.m.

schedule in their laboratory or office. If they are in the early stages—writing a grant for funding or doing research—they will probably be found using a computer at a desk.

During clinical trials, medical scientists work closely with doctors and other researchers. They might first test a drug on animals before human trials begin, so there are many possible scenarios for where this research takes place. And when the results are in, they will probably be back at a desk writing a report or analyzing the data.

There can be emotional ups and downs for medical scientists during each stage, depending on how their trial is going, but it is rarely dull or monotonous. As one researcher explains, "My job differs every day. We have about 30 different studies in progress at any time so I'm constantly reading and doing research in order to support my colleagues."[3]

Education and Training

Becoming a medical scientist usually takes eight to nine years of study after high school. This means a four-year college degree, usually in chemistry or biology, plus graduate school to earn a doctorate, which is also typically in biology. Students might be able to work as a research assistant to a medical scientist while studying for their doctoral degree.

Taking science classes in high school is a great way to begin on the path toward a medical science career. Classes in computer programing and statistics are very important as well. Designing studies and analyzing data using computers are critical parts of the medical scientist job, no matter the specialty. Being a good writer is also important. For example, public health scientists who focus on public health and disease prevention create written materials to educate the public.

Students who enjoy research and investigation may want to consider a career as a medical scientist. In this career, they can wear many hats while facing challenging medical mysteries. Some medical scientists say they considered going to medical school to become physicians, but they decided this field was better suited because they like solving problems and finding answers to scientific questions.

Skills and Personality

Patience and perseverance are two qualities that enable medical scientists to develop useful treatments and solve medical mysteries. Researching diseases, inventing new devices, or finding out why a person or a community has become sick takes perseverance. There is a lot of trial and error, so being resilient both intellectually and emotionally is necessary. As a medical scientist at the Institute of Cancer Research shares, "Science doesn't always go the way you want it—experiments fail and some of it is a grind, but every now and then you have a magic moment where you get a result and you say a-ha!"[4]

Details and analysis also matter in the world of medical science. Medical scientists need to be precise and double-check everything they do. They also need to be open-minded. There may be several ways to interpret a study or analyze data, so being able to see things from different angles is important.

Although most medical scientists work alone or with little supervision, they need to have good communication skills. They have to present theories, write proposals, and communicate their findings to colleagues and, sometimes, to nonscientists. During clinical trials, for instance, medical scientists may be called on to speak with patients or volunteers.

Other personality traits shared by medical scientists include caring about people and a desire to help improve lives. Many medical scientists talk about having a personal interest in a particular disease that may have affected a friend or a family member, and how this drives their research.

Working Conditions

Medical scientists usually work full-time, with a standard forty-hour workweek. The job is usually very safe, but sometimes they might work with a dangerous drug or chemical. This requires careful adherence to safety protocols.

A medical scientist prepares to conduct an experiment on a mouse. During clinical trials, medical scientists may test a drug on animals before human trials begin.

The Rewards of Research

"The future health, wealth and even survival of *Homo sapiens* depend on a deeper understanding of the laws and mechanisms of nature and on using this information to develop new technologies and therapies. For rationally thinking people with an altruistic bent, life can be no more rewarding than when practicing the scientific method for the benefit of all of the denizens of this fragile planet."

—Jonathan W. Yewdell, medical scientist

Jonathan W. Yewdell, "How to Succeed in Science: A Concise Guide for Young Biomedical Scientists," *Nature Reviews: Molecular Cell Biology*, vol. 9, no. 5, May 2008. www.ncbi.nlm.nih.gov.

Employers and Pay

Medical scientists can work in many places. Most work in hospitals and clinics that conduct medical studies or drug trials. They hold positions such as lab director or supervisor and may specialize in research in areas such as cancer, gerontology (the biology of aging), or neuroscience (the study of the brain). Some work in universities, where they teach and conduct research.

Other medical scientists are employed by pharmaceutical companies that are trying to develop new drugs and treatments. This can be more lucrative than working for the government or in a university or nonprofit research setting, but it also comes with more pressure to deliver products. Pharmaceutical companies only make money when their employees develop marketable products, so research is not just aimed at improving health but also at making a profit.

According to the Bureau of Labor Statistics (BLS), medical scientist jobs are mainly located on the East and West Coasts, where hospitals and colleges are found in the highest numbers. States with the highest concentrations of medical scientists are Massachusetts, Maryland, New York, Washington, and California.

Salaries for medical scientists vary depending on where they work, as seen in the 2018 BLS report. In the pharmaceutical industry, the average salary for medical scientists is about $115,000 a year. Medical scientists who work in laboratories and hospitals conducting research have an annual salary of between $85,000 and $90,000. On the lower end, colleges pay around $61,000 a year to those who teach and train future scientists in an academic setting.

What Is the Future Outlook for Medical Scientists?

Employment opportunities are good for medical scientists, with the BLS predicting 8 percent job growth by 2028. This is partly because Americans have become more and more dependent on drugs to treat a wide variety of ailments. In addition, there is an ongoing need for research into treatments for diseases such as acquired immune deficiency syndrome, cancer, and Alzheimer's disease. There is always a new frontier for medical research.

Find Out More

American Association for Cancer Research (AACR)
www.aacr.org

A major issue for medical scientists is research into cancer, and the AACR website has valuable information for professionals and students who have an interest in this area. The AACR has a foundation called Stand Up to Cancer, which offers volunteer opportunities.

American Society for Clinical Laboratory Science (ASCLS)
www.ascls.org

This ASCLS website provides information for scientists of all ages. It includes the section "Considering Careers in Laboratory Science" for students as well as links to scholarships and educational aids. It also offers a career center, which provides practical information, and online education opportunities.

Gerontological Society of America (GSA)

www.geron.org

The GSA is a unique organization. Its purpose is to promote collaboration between biologists, health professionals, policy makers, behavioral and social scientists, and other scientists. The GSA promotes healthy aging and believes this is possible when medical scientists and others work together.

National Institute of General Medical Sciences (NIGMS)

www.nigms.nih.gov

The website of the NIGMS is a treasure trove of information for anyone interested in the research that is being conducted today. It has links for undergraduate and doctoral study programs, research programs, and educational resources. A section on current news and events also makes this website a great source of information about advances in disease diagnosis, treatment, and prevention.

Physician Assistant

What Does a Physician Assistant Do?

Physician assistants (PAs) are licensed medical providers who, like physicians, work directly with their own patients. They examine, diagnose, and treat patients. But PAs are not physicians. Neither are they *assistants* to physicians nor *physicians'* assistants. They are sometimes called midlevel providers because they occupy a position somewhere between a nurse and a doctor in terms of training and authority. Physician assistants have more training and authority than nurses but less than doctors.

Despite the medical profession's long history, PAs have only been employed for about fifty years, when the position was created to improve and expand access to health care. Since that time, reports the American Academy of Physician Assistants (AAPA), the number of PAs practicing medicine in the United States has grown to more than 130,000.

Physician assistants work under a doctor's supervision. Although they interact directly with patients and independently evaluate and address patient needs, PAs routinely confer with supervising physicians. Most PAs say that they enjoy working with doctors as part of a team. As PA Candace Daugherty explains, "When I found out what the PA career was all about—being able to participate in the diagnostic and treatment portions of patient care . . . and having a supervising MD who I work with as a team—I knew I had found my fit."[5]

Physician assistants work in all areas of medicine, including primary care, pediatrics, emergency medicine, surgery, psychiatry, orthopedics, and cardiology. Within each of these specialties, the PAs' day-to-day job has many of the same components. They examine patients and talk with them about their medical history. They work to build good relationships with patients and help guide them to better health, developing treatment plans as needed. They also perform procedures, such as setting a broken bone, and some also assist in surgery. Daugherty says it is a rewarding job: "I get to see everything I would want to, including complex medical cases. I get to perform procedures daily."[6]

In rural areas, which often have few or no doctors, PAs provide most of the patient care. In this way, thousands of people who might otherwise not have access to a local primary care physician can get care without having to travel long distances. Because of this, PAs are sometimes called physician extenders.

People who work as PAs in emergency rooms (ERs) describe their job as both challenging and rewarding. People without insurance sometimes end up in the ER because they have nowhere else to go for medical treatment. Physician assistants treat patients with a wide variety of medical issues that might have been preventable if the patient had had a primary care physician. "At times it becomes a hard job because we are left to handle a lot of the population that falls through the cracks,"[7] says Daugherty, but she and other PAs enjoy the excitement of the ER and would recommend this career. According to the AAPA, 96 percent of PAs in all specialties report that they love their job.

The Workday

Physician assistants who live in larger towns and cities typically work in a medical office or a clinic as part of a team that includes doctors, nurses, and support staff. They see patients by appointment or as walk-ins in an ER. Those who work in rural areas usually have a much smaller team and may have to confer with other medical professionals by phone or video conference.

Patient visits with PAs are similar to doctor-patient visits. Physician assistants begin by talking with patients about their medical history and the reason for the visit. If the patient is there for a routine checkup rather than an illness or injury, the PA will do a wellness exam and possibly order routine lab tests. If the patient has come to the clinic because of an illness or injury, the PA will do an exam and order tests (such as blood work, X-rays, or an ultrasound) that will help determine the right diagnosis. Once they reach a diagnosis, the PA will recommend a course of treatment. Throughout this process, the PA will often consult with their supervising physician.

The PA's workday also includes administrative tasks. Like all medical professionals, PAs keep records on all interactions with patients. Their day might also include writing prescriptions as well as referrals for patients who need to see specialists. Physician assistants must also read medical journals to keep up with the latest medical treatments and other information about health care.

Education and Training

Students must earn several degrees to become a PA. After high school, they must first earn a bachelor's degree. There are many areas of study that future PAs can pursue in college, but most focus on science and psychology. This is the first step toward becoming a PA.

Many PAs already work as registered nurses, paramedics, emergency medical technicians, or in other medical fields before they apply to PA school. This experience is valued by the PA schools because it shows that the person has an aptitude for working with people in a clinical setting.

The PA program results in a master's degree. There are currently more than 230 accredited PA programs in the United States. It takes an average of twenty-seven months of full-time study to complete the program. The program includes both classroom

Beads and Bugs and Boils

"I love being a PA. I love the procedures that I do. I like suturing and fixing dislocated fingers and shoulders. I love pulling beads and bugs out of patient's ears and I love opening up boils and cleaning the infection inside them. This sounds gross to many people, but I really find those procedures to be satisfying.

    The thing that I love the most about being a PA though is trying to help people. I try to really listen carefully and thoughtfully to every patient that I see. I try to treat them as if they were in my family. I think to myself, 'If this were my mom (brother, sister, etc.) how would I evaluate and treat them?'"

—Tess Messer, physician assistant

Quoted in Job Shadow, "An Interview with Physician Assistant Tess Meyer." https://jobshadow.com.

coursework and supervised clinical work. One of the biggest appeals of PA school is that the program is much shorter than medical school, but PAs can provide many of the same services as doctors. Classroom study focuses on anatomy, physiology, clinical medicine, pharmacology, ethics, and diagnostic skills. This is followed by two thousand hours of clinical experience, with rotations in different specialties, such as family, pediatric, and emergency medicine.

After graduation from PA school, candidates must pass a certification exam and obtain a license from the state where they will practice. PAs are lifelong learners, always expanding their knowledge and skills.

Skills and Personality

Compassion is one of the most important qualities of a PA. Working to understand the needs and concerns of patients is the key to building trusting relationships. Being perceptive and a good listener goes hand in hand with this trait. Sometimes patients are embarrassed or have trouble explaining what is happening in their lives. They are much more likely to be honest and feel comfortable talking to a PA who is compassionate.

Nothing Is Routine for a Patient

"I realized how our 'routines' each day mean so much more to our patients we serve. The smile, the thoroughness of the workup, and the extra mile we are willing to go on behalf of our patients, truly make the difference between an ordinary clinician and an exceptional clinician. I am often ordinary in other areas, but how I treat patients in my realm of expertise and knowledge has always been a No. 1 priority."

—Tajuana D. Lordeus, physician assistant

Quoted in Sara Seng, "My PA Story: Tajuana D. Lordeus," *Barton Blog,* Barton Associates, October 7, 2015. www.bartonassociates.com.

Physician assistants must also be logical and good problem solvers, able to take in complex information and figure out a plan of action. They must be able to deal with pressure and stress and remain grounded in all situations. They must make decisions with confidence and have good judgment.

Because they see patients independently but are part of a team, PAs must be able to work well alone and with others. Working alone requires the ability to handle a significant amount of responsibility. But the job of the PA also requires good communication and cooperation with a supervising physician and other health professionals.

Working Conditions

Physician assistants work in offices or clinics that are usually very comfortable and well supported. They are supervised by a doctor, and this relationship is typically collaborative. There is a mutual respect between doctors and PAs, and they each have their own job and responsibilities.

Most PAs work forty hours a week or more. Some PAs work nights, weekends, and holidays, especially if they work in a hospital. The job can be physically demanding; most PAs are on their feet making rounds, and they may have to assist patients. The job also can be emotionally demanding because PAs develop strong relationships with their patients and grow to care about them and their families. Jeffrey Katz, the former president of the AAPA, has been a PA for over twenty years. He believes that long-term connections are the best part of his job: "It is really cool to see the children of children [I've treated]. I don't think there's any better gift,"[8] he says.

Employers and Pay

In 2018, 55 percent of PAs worked in doctors' offices, and 26 percent worked in hospitals, according to the Bureau of Labor Statistics (BLS). Physician assistants have a unique relationship with their employer because they are under contract with the supervising physician. The physician does not have to be present at all times, and the amount of supervision a PA is required to have varies from state to state.

Salaries for PAs vary by specialty and also by region. The average reported by the BLS's *Occupational Outlook Handbook* was $108,610 for all PAs, with a range of $70,000 to $151,000. In general, surgical PAs earn more than those who work in a more general field such as family medicine. There are also many high-paying opportunities in rural America. The BLS reports that some of the most highly paid PAs work in Alaska, Wyoming, Montana, and rural sections of Texas and Louisiana.

What Is the Future Outlook for Physician Assistants?

Career opportunities for PAs are booming. The BLS projects a 31 percent increase in demand for PAs by the year 2028, which is much higher than the average for all careers. At least three-quarters of all PAs receive multiple job offers when they graduate, according to the AAPA website, so PAs have many choices about where to live and work.

Health care is moving toward more efficient, team-based practices, and PAs are a vital part of this trend. Physician assistants can deliver routine and preventive care, which is why they are in such great demand. According to an AAPA survey, over 90 percent of patients said PAs are trusted providers and improve the quality of health care.

Find Out More

American Academy of Physician Assistants (AAPA)
www.aapa.org

The AAPA website provides news and career information for PAs, includes a section for interested students, and posts short, informative videos on a wide range of topics. The academy also hosts workshops and other events.

Physician Assistant Education Association (PAEA)
https://paeaonline.org

The PAEA website is dedicated to helping people find educational resources and support if they are interested in becoming a PA. The association holds workshops, provides assistance with tests and applications, and has information about current issues that affect people wishing to become PAs.

PhysicianAssistantEDU.org
https://www.physicianassistantedu.org

This is a great resource for students interested in finding up-to-date information about how to become a PA, with specific information for each state in the United States. There are sections on education, careers, and certifications.

Physician Assistant Life
https://www.thepalife.com

This site is divided into three sections: one for pre-PA students, one for current PA students, and the last for PAs currently working. It offers resources and advice for all levels. It also includes a blog in which PAs discuss their jobs and give advice to potential PAs.

Prosthetist

What Does a Prosthetist Do?

When an active eleven-year-old boy is diagnosed with bone cancer of the knee, he thinks about all the things he may no longer be able to do: basketball, football, swimming, horseback riding, and so much more. Surgery removes the diseased bone, which can lead to amputation and the need for an artificial limb. When this happened to Steven Miller, he and his family made many four-hour car trips for treatment, but his first artificial device did not fit well. Miller recalls taking it off at night and having blisters and pain and becoming depressed. Then they found a new prosthetist who made him a properly designed prosthetic. He recalls, "It was like night and day . . . to have a really good-fitting prosthesis. . . . I could run, play, and do sports, and I wasn't in pain all the time. That's what triggered [me] to go into prosthetics, knowing how a prosthetist can really affect someone's life."[9]

Health professionals who make artificial limbs for people are called prosthetists. This is a dynamic and growing allied health career. Prosthetists work with people who have been born without a limb, have lost a limb during an accident or during military service, or had a limb amputated because of a medical condition. The artificial limbs

A Few Facts

Number of Jobs
9,100

Pay
Average salary of $69,120 in 2018

Educational Requirements
Master's degree

Personal Qualities
Detail oriented, compassionate, patient, caring, inquisitive, dexterous

Work Settings
Medical supply manufacturers, clinics, hospitals

Future Job Outlook
20 percent increase by 2028

Giving Hope

"I have treated patients who have come to me in a state of hopelessness. Many are new amputees or amputees who have not had a good experience elsewhere. Being an amputee myself, I totally understand their situation. I work extremely hard with each patient to ensure each one becomes a success story. Seeing a patient come into my practice in a wheelchair, working with the patient to ensure the fabrication of a well-fitting, state-of-the-art prosthesis, and watching the patient walk, is incredibly satisfying and rewarding."

—Brooke Artesi, prosthetist

Quoted in American Academy of Orthotics and Prosthetics, "Spotlighting Women in O & P: Brooke Artesi, CPO/LPO." www.oandp.org.

they make are called prostheses and can include arms, hands, legs, and feet.

Prosthetists make and fit these artificial body parts with the goal of helping patients live productive and independent lives. Prostheses have to be strong and durable. Most importantly, they have to do the work of the missing limb. So, when a prosthetist designs an artificial leg or foot, it has to allow the patient to stand, walk, and even run or jump. When a prosthetist designs an artificial arm or hand, it has to allow the person to reach, grab, and perform activities of daily living such as eating, writing, and dressing.

The Workday

For a prosthetist working in a clinic, the day might start by seeing a new patient who has been referred by a physician. The prosthetist examines the patient and measures the area that needs an artificial limb. The prosthetist learns about the patient's lifestyle and his or her needs and hopes for the new limb. The prosthetist also tests the patient's muscle strength and range of motion in the area where the prosthesis will be attached. When creating an artificial limb, the prosthetist considers these factors as well as how much is left of the existing limb.

Next, the prosthetist makes a model of the area where the artificial limb will be attached. This involves using plaster to make a cast and a mold of the existing limb to which the artificial limb will connect. The prosthetist creates a design for the prosthesis and selects materials for the socket, usually plastic or carbon fiber. Once the prosthesis is constructed, the prosthetist meets with the patient again to fit and adjust the new limb. For an artificial foot or knee, the socket goes over the existing limb. Arm and hand prostheses can be more complicated, involving a processor that can read electrical signals as well as a motor and battery inside the prosthesis that enable movement. Some artificial limbs even have a thin layer of silicone on the outside that looks like skin, and the prosthetist can add freckles, veins, and even little hairs to make it look more realistic. They show the patient how to use and care for their prosthesis and talk to them to be sure they are happy and comfortable.

Other prosthetists do not work with patients directly; instead, they specialize in the construction and sale of prosthetic devices. Their workday is spent in a manufacturing plant or at a medical supply company. In these facilities, prosthetists might fulfill custom orders. They might also make products that are mass marketed for use with prostheses, such as special socks known as "stump socks," which cover the existing limb and provide a cushion between the skin and the prosthesis.

Education and Training

To become a prosthetist, a student must obtain both a bachelor's and a master's degree. This usually takes about six years in total after high school. The bachelor's degree can be in any subject, but it should include classes in science and math. Master's programs in prosthetics include classes in anatomy, physiology, materials science, neuroscience, and kinesiology. These classes help the student understand the human body and how it moves, as well as the properties of materials used in making artificial limbs. In addition to academic classes, there is a clinical component during which the student works as a resident with a practicing prosthetist for one year.

After receiving the master's degree, a prosthetist applies for a license. Most prosthetists are also certified by the American Board for Certification in Orthotics, Prosthetics & Pedorthotics.

Skills and Personality

A successful prosthetist needs to have many qualities, but the most important ones are the desire to help people and inquisitiveness. No two patients are the same, and the prosthetist has to work with each patient to create a unique plan. Prosthetists say they enjoy being able to tangibly help patients—for example, enabling them to walk or dress themselves once again.

People who have lost a limb experience many emotions and are likely struggling to adjust to this loss. A kind, caring, and empathetic prosthetist can help them adjust to this huge life change. Being a prosthetist takes patience because it can be a long process to design and fit an artificial limb, taking weeks or even months from start to finish. Good communication skills are also essential as a prosthetist must connect with and listen to patients and be able to teach them about their prosthetic limb.

This is a field that might appeal to someone who enjoys building or working with their hands. Dexterity is a critical skill when designing or constructing a new limb. Attention to detail and accuracy are also necessary skills. A prosthetist must take precise measurements to ensure that the artificial limb fits well. When fitting an artificial limb, small adjustments can make a big difference. A willingness to adapt and to search for just the right fit are important skills for the job. Prosthetist Phil Stevens explains how sometimes "we realize that if we took another quarter-inch off that foot plate, it would fit in the shoe a little easier . . . and we give that wrench another quarter-turn to see

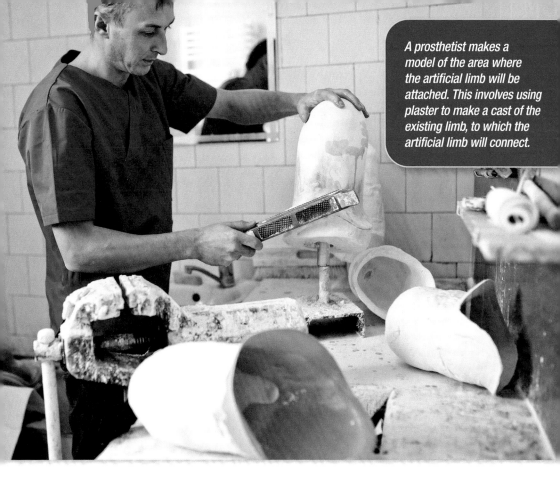

A prosthetist makes a model of the area where the artificial limb will be attached. This involves using plaster to make a cast of the existing limb, to which the artificial limb will connect.

if we can't improve the alignment."[10] Poorly fitting prostheses can cause irritation or even pain, so prosthetists must be willing to keep working and adjusting until the artificial limb fits perfectly.

Working Conditions

Prosthetists usually work full-time with regular hours and little to no overtime or weekend requirements. Most work in either a manufacturing setting or in an office where patients are seen by appointment. In an office setting, they might see eight to twelve patients a day on average. If they have a particularly complicated case, they could spend an entire day with just one patient.

People wonder whether it is depressing to work with people who have lost limbs, but 85 percent of prosthetists say that it is very rewarding, and they enjoy their work. "It's a very inspiring place to spend the day," Stevens shares. "Patients come in with overwhelming challenges, and we get to help them overcome them."[11] Many practitioners say it is very satisfying to form long-term relationships with their patients as they work with them to repair or replace their artificial limb through the years.

Working conditions are considered to be comfortable, and working as part of a team means prosthetists have professional support and camaraderie in the workplace. A prosthetist does need to be in good enough physical condition to move freely, bend to measure a patient, or help them walk. They work with tools and equipment, so they must take basic safety precautions at times, such as wearing goggles, gloves, or masks.

Employers and Pay

About one-third of practicing prosthetists work for a company that makes medical equipment. Other prosthetists work in hospitals or in private offices or clinics, many of which specialize in treating amputees. The American Academy of Orthotists and Prosthetists reports that in 2018, 100 percent of professionals in this field were employed.

Salaries for prosthetists range from approximately $40,000 to over $108,000, depending on experience. The average salary is $69,120, according to the Bureau of Labor Statistics (BLS) in 2018. Prosthetists earn the highest salaries in California, Michigan, New York, Illinois, and Texas, with an average annual salary in California of $88,000.

What Is the Future Outlook for Prosthetists?

Prosthetists are in huge demand, with expected job growth of 20 percent by 2028, according to the BLS. There are currently not enough certified prosthetists to meet the demand in the United States, and some professional organizations report that one-third of the people who need an artificial limb have to wait up to a year for appropriate care. Many prosthetists choose to work with one

Extraordinary Challenges

"It's sometimes a challenge to help individuals recognize and understand that this new reality will not define them. In my mind, these folks are extraordinary, demonstrating phenomenal strength, determination and courage. It's quite humbling to be a part of this rehabilitation process."

—Catherine Trenchard, prosthetist

Quoted in Robin L. Flanigan, "Life Changing Work Comes Naturally for Prosthetics Practitioner," *Rochester (NY) Democrat & Chronicle*, January 15, 2018. www.democratandchronicle.com.

population, such as in a cancer center or with veterans who have lost limbs in combat. But no matter where they choose to work, prosthetists know that their work is valuable and appreciated. In the past, people had to learn to live without a limb, but today they have more options and can lead better lives because of the advancements in making artificial limbs and the skills of trained prosthetists.

Find Out More

American Academy of Orthotists and Prosthetists (AAOP)
https://www.oandp.org

The AAOP website is a great resource for seeing what professionals in this field are currently doing. There is information about research, education, and advocacy for prosthetists. There is also information for students or potential students.

Limbs4Life
https://www.limbs4life.org.au

This Australian site offers information from the patient's viewpoint. There are inspiring and interesting stories of people who have suffered the loss of a limb and how they have recovered. Peer support, information about medical options and prosthetics, and current research can be found here.

National Association for the Advancement of Orthotics & Prosthetics (NAAOP)

https://naaop.org

NAAOP provides education about how prosthetics and orthotics are regulated. It advocates for patients and shares stories about how patients can get the help they need.

National Commission on Orthotic and Prosthetic Education (NCOPE)

http://www.ncope.org

The NCOPE website has helpful information for anyone interested in a career in orthotics or prosthetics, where they can assist in making braces or artificial limbs. Its focus is on education as well as sharing current news and information.

Nurse Anesthetist

A Few Facts

Number of Jobs
45,000

Pay
Average salary of
$167,950 in 2018

Educational Requirements
Registered nurse license
and master's degree

Personal Qualities
Strong communication
and critical-thinking
skills, compassionate,
detail oriented

Work Settings
Hospitals (emergency,
obstetrics, surgical
departments), doctors'
offices, outpatient clinics

Future Job Outlook
17 percent increase by
2028

What Does a Nurse Anesthetist Do?

A nurse anesthetist (NA) is a registered nurse (RN) who has obtained additional training to provide anesthesia to patients who are having an operation or other medical procedure. Anesthesia is used to numb a specific part of the body or to make a patient sleep during surgery. When only a part of the body is made numb, this is called a local anesthetic. In this case, the patient remains awake and alert, but the area being worked on is "asleep," and the patient does not feel anything. Local anesthetics may be administered by injection or with a spray or ointment that is applied to the area. For more involved procedures, including many surgeries, patients are put to sleep so that they are unconscious and unaware of the work being done. This is called general anesthesia. Nurse anesthetists use intravenous drugs or inhaled gases for this type of anesthesia. In both cases, it is the job of the nurse anesthetist to make sure patients are safe and comfortable.

The NA stays by the patient's side throughout the entire procedure, ensuring the patient does not feel pain and monitoring his or her vital signs. Vital signs include a person's pulse, blood pressure, breathing, and temperature. Because surgery is invasive and requires incisions, a loss of blood or other complications can seriously affect a person's vital signs and overall health. It is the NA's job to inform the surgeon about any observed changes and adjust the anesthesia to keep the patient stable. Big changes in blood pressure, temperature, or breathing can lead to serious problems and even death. When the surgery is finished, the NA gradually stops administering the anesthesia and guides the patient back to consciousness.

In some states, nurse anesthetists work with patients under the direction of an anesthesiologist, or a doctor trained in the use of anesthesia. In other states, and in many rural communities, nurse anesthetists work independently but must still review and discuss their cases with an anesthesiologist. In both environments, they must become a certified registered nurse anesthetist (CRNA).

A Typical Workday

Nurse anesthetists usually work with patients before, during, and after their procedure. These three phases of patient care are known as preoperative, intraoperative, and postoperative. The time spent on each phase varies from case to case, but NAs see each patient through every step.

The preoperative phase is before an operation. Nurse anesthetists gather basic patient information, such as age, medical history, allergies, height and weight, and current medications. They also ask about drug or alcohol use and other medical issues. This is important because some health conditions pose risks to a patient's health when that person is under anesthesia. This initial information-gathering session helps the NA determine which drugs are safest to use and whether to give them intravenously or through a breathing mask. A good rapport between patients and NAs is important so that patients feel comfortable and give honest answers to these questions.

Making Awful Moments a Little Better

"Part of the satisfaction of providing anesthesia is the ability to help someone through possibly the worst day in his or her life. They are afraid of the diagnosis, they are afraid of the impending pain, and all of the unknowns that lie before them. Your presence as a calming entity at their bedside at that very moment becomes paramount. The fact that you possess the knowledge and skills to see them safely through their procedure is secondary; the humanity that you bring to their life is what becomes more important than any medication you can administer."

—Valerie Bell, nurse anesthetist

Quoted in Kaitlin Louie, "Interview with Valerie Bell, DNP, CRNA—Certified Registered Nurse Anesthetist," Online FNP Programs. www.onlinefnpprograms.com.

The intraoperative phase comes next. This is when patients have their procedures and the NA makes sure they are comfortable. In some cases, NAs may have to insert tubes, known as airway equipment, down the throats of their patients to help them breathe. This process is known as intubation. This tube is held in place by other equipment and is usually connected to a ventilator, which is a machine that breathes for the patient during their procedure. Kelsey Horton, a CRNA, describes this part of her workday:

When I first get to work, I get my room set up for the day. This includes checking my anesthesia machine and making sure all components are working. I get my airway equipment ready and drugs drawn up that I will be using for the case. I take my patient back to the operating room, induce them under anesthesia, and intubate them for the case if necessary. Throughout the procedure I monitor the patient's vital signs, administer a variety of medications, manage the ventilator, and keep them asleep and happy.[12]

The final stage is postoperative, which begins when patients go to recovery. During recovery, NAs stay with their patients to make sure their vital signs are steady and their pain is controlled while they wake up. They sometimes visit the patients later that day or the next, if needed.

Most NAs agree that their work is very satisfying, as Horton shares: "Patients are often very nervous or anxious before having major surgery. I love to make a connection with them and gain their trust that I will take excellent care of them while they are under anesthesia. When they wake up pain free, without nausea, and thank me for taking care of them I always feel very accomplished and proud of my profession."[13]

Education and Training

Nurse anesthetists are RNs who have obtained a master of science degree in nursing, specializing in anesthesiology. Before applying to become an NA, an RN must work for at least one year in a critical-care setting such as an intensive care unit. This requirement gives the applicant hands-on experience with patients who have life-threatening conditions and need constant care. Nurse anesthetist programs are academically challenging and require a full-time commitment. Current NAs recall having to study fifty to sixty hours per week in order to succeed in their classes.

Finally, NAs must pass a national examination to receive their CRNA certification. Most states also require their own state license to practice.

Skills and Personality

Nurse anesthetists have to be strong communicators. They have important conversations with patients before and after their procedures. During procedures, an NA has to communicate critical information to the medical team.

Nurse anesthetists must have excellent critical-thinking skills to quickly assess and respond to their patients' needs. Being detail oriented and having a good memory are also very important characteristics. Nurse anesthetists must be meticulous when calculating and measuring medications. They also have to remember lots of facts about the many medicines they dispense.

There are many personal qualities that make a good NA. The ability to empathize and comfort patients and their families is key. People are vulnerable when they (or a family member) are facing surgery. According to a study that appeared a few years ago in the *Saudi Journal of Anesthesia*, over half (56 percent) of surgical patients fear they will not wake up from surgery, and 73 percent are afraid that they will be awake or aware during surgery. Patience and kindness are also traits that patients say they value. Since every day and every patient bring new challenges, a person with a flexible, positive personality would be well suited for this career.

Working Conditions

There really is no "typical" workday for an NA. At hospitals, they work nights, weekends, holidays, and sometimes twenty-four-hour shifts. A CRNA working in a medical office will likely have more regular hours. CRNA Wallena Gould asks new NAs this question:

> What type of lifestyle do you want? A Level I trauma center provides lots of opportunities to work and make considerable overtime if you want to. Some people want a local hospital . . . where it is less stressful. Some CRNAs work at surgery centers that are only open from 7 [a.m.] to 4 [p.m.], no on-call and no weekends. So, it depends on what lifestyle you want once you graduate.[14]

There can be physical and emotional stress in this profession. When monitoring a patient during a long operation, NAs might be on their feet for hours. Patient complications during anesthesia, such as difficulty breathing or a dropping heart rate, can threaten the patient's life. The NA must act quickly and calmly to stabilize the patient's condition. In all settings, NAs report that they get tremendous satisfaction from this career.

Employers and Pay

Nurse anesthetists have many employment options. Most CRNAs work in hospitals, but others get jobs at dental offices or clinics specializing in outpatient plastic surgery, podiatry, and ophthalmology. Still other CRNAs work with men and women in the US armed services.

The average annual salary for a nurse anesthetist is $167,950, according to the Bureau of Labor Statistics (BLS), which is significantly higher than other types of nurses. In addition, CRNAs are better paid because they have more training and more responsibility (and thus more liability) than most other nursing specialties. The BLS reports some of the highest salaries in large metropolitan areas, with three California cities (San Francisco, San Diego, and Oakland) all offering salaries above $230,000. The BLS also reports that rural states like Montana and Wyoming offer salaries in the $250,000 per year range to entice NAs there.

What Is the Future Outlook for Nurse Anesthetists?

The future is one of opportunity for NAs. Job opportunities are expected to increase by 17 percent by 2028, according to the BLS. A CRNA can do many of the same things as a physician anesthesiologist. This can be more cost-effective for insurers and hospitals because a CRNA's salary is significantly lower than the salary of an anesthesiologist.

The demand for CRNAs is partly due to the shortage of anesthesiologists, especially at inner-city hospitals and rural clinics. Some states report that nearly 100 percent of their anesthesia is provided by NAs because there are no anesthesiologists in the area. In two-thirds of rural hospitals, CRNAs are the sole providers of anesthesia, allowing these rural hospitals to perform lifesaving surgeries, according to the Hospital Careers website. Anyone studying to become an NA will find a lucrative and rewarding career at the end of their studies. As CRNA Frank Gerbasi says, "I've been a CRNA for 35 years, it's a great profession. I've never met a CRNA that regretted going into the field."[15]

Find Out More

American Association of Colleges of Nursing (AACN)
www.aacnnursing.org

The AACN website is meant for students looking for information about undergraduate and graduate nursing education, career options in nursing, and ways to seek financial aid to help pay for nursing school. There is a section on policy and advocacy and an interesting article on the nurse shortage.

American Association of Nurse Anesthetists
www.aana.com

This is the website of the AANA, a professional organization that represents NAs. It is full of information for current or aspiring professionals as well as a section with articles for patients. This is a great place to find a wide variety of information and insight.

Nurse.org
https://nurse.org

This website has an easy-to-read, user-friendly format to find out about nursing. A blog contains real, honest posts from NAs and other nursing professionals. It also includes information about education and scholarships available to prospective nurses.

Nurse Practitioner Schools
www.nursepractitionerschools.com

This website is a great place for students to get step-by-step instructions and information about how to become an NA as well as other specialties in nursing. There are links to other relevant sites as well as a section for frequently asked questions.

Medical Services Manager

What Does a Medical Services Manager Do?

When people visit the doctor because they are sick, their only concern is getting better. They may not give much thought to who runs the office and makes sure that their appointment is on time, their forms are filled out correctly, their records are kept confidential, the nurses and support staff are well trained, and their insurance is billed. But all of these details are important, and having a person who manages these details allows doctors to focus on their patients. The people who do this job are called medical services managers; they take care of the business side of health care. They plan, direct, and coordinate the behind-the-scenes activities that allow hospitals, doctors' offices, and other medical facilities to function.

At a hospital, a medical services manager oversees a department such as information technology, finance, or human resources. There likely will be several medical services managers working together to run a large practice or facility. In a small practice, one medical services manager often is in charge of every aspect of running a doctor's office. Karen Blanchette, who is the director of the Professional Association of Health Care Office Management, explains that for a medical

---

A Few Facts

Number of Jobs
406,100

Pay
Average salary of
$99,730 in 2018

Educational Requirements
Bachelor's degree

Personal Qualities
Logical, analytical, detail oriented, trustworthy

Work Settings
Office environment in hospitals, clinics, and health care facilities

Future Job Outlook
18 percent increase by 2028

services manager overseeing a practice, "the responsibilities are numerous and varied, covering all administrative aspects of running a medical business. It's your job to run a practice that's efficient, compliant, and profitable."[16]

Medical services managers are sometimes called health information managers because a key part of their job is to either create or manage the practice's system for managing, organizing, and analyzing patient health data. This data includes patient health histories, notes from appointments, test results, diagnoses, and treatment plans. Such systems are almost 100 percent electronic. They must be both accurate and secure.

All patient information is personal and confidential. But there are times when some of this information has to be shared—either with other health care providers or with insurance companies. The medical services manager is responsible for making sure that when patient information is shared, it is done properly. One example of this is when patients need to have their medical information released for treatment, perhaps at a rehab facility or a behavioral health center. Medical services managers need to be sure everything the office records, saves, and sends out regarding their patients is accurate and complete.

The Workday

The typical workday of a medical services manager is busy and varied. "What's so fun and exciting about the field—it's not the same day after day. If you work in a small facility, as a health information manager, you will wear multiple hats,"[17] says health information director Jane Duckert. In addition to setting up and/or maintaining a data management system, medical services managers oversee many other aspects of the department or office. They might be responsible for scheduling and giving ongoing training to the support and administrative staff in the practice. When there is turnover, they are often responsible for recruiting and training new hires. They supervise the staff and serve as a go-between for the office staff and the medical staff. Billing for the services

"The Greater Good"

"I think everybody should be working for the greater good. I never wanted to work directly with patients, but always knew that the work that I did could make a big difference. The better I did my job, the better caregivers could do their jobs. I think you could have the kind of impact as close to or as far from the patient as you want and still be making a difference. Students should never forget that there's a patient at the end of whatever work they are doing."

—Cheryl Martin, chief knowledge officer for the American Health Information Management Association

Quoted in Nina Chamlou, "Protecting Patient Data—an Interview with AHIMA's Cheryl Martin," Medical Technology Schools. www.medicaltechnologyschools.com.

provided by the doctor or hospital is one of the manager's most important duties because this money pays the salaries of everyone working in the practice. This can be complex because it often involves insurance companies. Many medical services managers talk with insurance companies on a daily basis.

Meetings are a necessary, if not always well-loved, part of most jobs, and the medical services manager career is no exception. Managers might meet with their team to talk about how to improve efficiency or any quality-of-care issues that the hospital or doctor's office might be dealing with. Some examples of this could be issues with patient wait times, accuracy in record keeping, or compliance with Medicare. Making a schedule is also a part of the job, so managers meet with the leaders of the practice to ensure that the schedule is working for them and their patients.

Record keeping and budgeting are two more aspects of the medical services manager's job. They have to keep records of all the equipment and supplies, pay bills, and generally make sure everyone in the office has what they need to do their jobs. The manager also oversees patient billing, fees that are charged for services, and reimbursements from insurance companies.

Medical services managers take care of the business side of health care. They plan, direct, and coordinate the behind-the-scenes activities that allow medical facilities to function.

Education and Training

Medical services managers typically have bachelor's degrees in health management or business administration. Because the job touches so many different areas, students usually take a diverse array of classes, including accounting, medical terminology, law and ethics, health information services, and budgeting. Strong technical skills are necessary in this field, so any and all computer classes that teach coding and software programs and systems would be beneficial. Some people pursue master's degrees, although work experience is as important (and sometimes more important) when it comes to career advancement.

Skills and Personality

A career as a medical services manager is primarily an office job that would best suit a person who wants a job with clearly defined duties. The ability to use logic and reasoning to find solutions is very important. Strong analytical skills are also needed when deciding how to best organize and evaluate large amounts of patient data. Medical services managers must be very detail oriented because even a small mistake could be costly to the patient or to the practice if not corrected. Computer skills are also necessary. In smaller practices, medical services managers may have to set up the computers and design the system the office staff uses for day-to-day tasks. In a hospital or nursing home, they need to navigate complex computer systems used by whatever department they are involved with, such as billing, scheduling, accounting, or personnel.

Good communication skills are also essential. Medical services managers must be able to speak with doctors, support staff, and representatives of insurance companies. Sometimes patients can become upset, for example, when dealing with a claim that is denied by their insurance company. This can be stressful for the medical services manager trying to help, so the ability to stay calm under pressure is also valuable.

A high level of integrity is also of the utmost importance. Medical services managers are privy to confidential patient information and are responsible for protecting it. As Cheryl Martin, who holds a master's degree in health information management, explains, "Patients trust us. Whether it's just no-big-deal data, or it's something that could be devastating if other people knew, it really shouldn't matter. Patients perhaps don't know where their data is . . . but they trust us to keep that data safe."[18]

Working Conditions

Medical services managers might run an entire medical practice, or they might work in one department in a hospital, but no matter where they work, they have a lot of responsibility. They usually have a comfortable, private office. They are part of a team and may manage the staff who work in a practice or department, and they report to the doctor who owns the practice or to hospital leadership. There are usually frequent, regular meetings with coworkers to be sure that the office or department is running smoothly or to introduce any new systems. They also meet to discuss the frequently changing laws and regulations that impact health care. Blanchette says, "It can be stressful keeping up with the changes in an industry that's as highly regulated as health care. That's why professional networks and resources . . . are so critical for success."[19]

A standard forty-hour workweek is common, with overtime only rarely needed. The exception to this would be for medical services managers who work in facilities that provide twenty-four-hour care, such as a nursing home. These managers may have to work nighttime and weekend shifts to ensure coverage at all times.

Employers and Pay

There are many different locations in need of medical services managers. These include hospitals, long-term care facilities (such as nursing homes), insurance companies, pharmaceutical companies, public health agencies, and doctors' offices.

Around 40 percent of medical services management jobs are within hospitals, according to the Bureau of Labor Statistics (BLS). It takes many skilled staff members to manage and organize everything necessary to keep hospitals running smoothly. The BLS reports that about 20 percent work in clinics and doctors' offices, with the remainder working in nursing homes or for governmental departments that are connected with health care.

There is a wide range of salaries for medical services managers, determined mainly by experience. The range reported by the BLS is between $58,680 and $182,600 each year, with an average salary of $99,730 in 2018.

What Is the Future Outlook for Medical Services Managers?

The health care industry is expanding, mainly because people in the United States are living longer. This has increased the need for doctors and hospitals—and medical services managers are needed to work behind the scenes to manage this growth. The field is expected to grow by 18 percent by 2028, according to the BLS. Strong leadership is needed to manage these hospitals and medical facilities. Doctors and nurses are on the front line, but medical services managers are a vital, if less recognizable, part of the health care system.

Find Out More

American Health Information Management Association (AHIMA)

www.ahima.org

AHIMA supports professionals in the field and also people who want to learn more about how professionals manage health information. Its website includes sections with current health topics as well as a section for students and a career center.

Commission on Accreditation for Health Informatics and Information Management Education (CAHIIM)
www.cahiim.org

CAHIIM is a professional organization that offers accreditation for people working in medical services management. Its website also has a lot of information for students. This is an interesting resource to learn about the continuing educational and social opportunities in this field.

HealthCarePathway.com
www.healthcarepathway.com

This is an excellent site for information about the career opportunities for students to pursue in health care. Careers are arranged by the level of education needed. The section "Health Informatics and Business" includes information about medical services managers.

Genetic Counselor

What Does a Genetic Counselor Do?

As the name indicates, genetic counselors are trained in two areas—genetics and counseling. Genetics is the study of genes and inheritance. Many human characteristics are determined by the DNA in the genes people inherit from their parents. The codes that determine the way a person looks or certain characteristics like eye and hair color, which hand is dominant, and how a person ages are contained in sections of deoxyribonucleic acid (DNA) called genes. Some genes and gene mutations can increase the chance of developing certain diseases. Some people choose to undergo genetic testing to determine the likelihood of developing a genetic disease or of passing it on to their children.

The job of genetic counselors is twofold. First, they discuss the risks and benefits of genetic testing with people who are thinking about undergoing these tests. Second, they are responsible for clearly explaining the test results. Those who do this job must have a strong understanding of genetics and be able to clearly communicate genetic inheritance to people who might have little or no knowledge of this subject. Genetic counselors must also be able to help

A Few Facts

Number of Jobs
3,000

Pay
Average salary of
$80,370 in 2018

Educational Requirements
Master's degree

Personal Qualities
Inquisitive, good communicator, sensitive, trustworthy, logical

Work Settings
Hospitals, labs, doctors' offices, universities

Future Job Outlook
27 percent increase by 2028

people deal with uncomfortable or scary test results and talk with them about their choices regarding how to proceed. Some have even described the job of genetic counselor as part biology teacher and part therapist because they teach but they also listen and advise. Joy Larsen Haidle says she sees her job as a genetic counselor as a "great blend of science, critical thinking, psychology and counseling."[20]

The Workday

Genetic counselors spend their days meeting with patients for a variety of reasons. At an initial appointment, they might talk at length with patients and family members about what they hope to learn from genetic testing. Having realistic expectations about what testing can show is important. Counselors will also urge patients to think about what they want to do once they have the test results. For instance, a genetic counselor might encourage a couple to discuss ahead of time whether to have a baby if they find they are at high risk for passing on a birth defect.

There are other topics to discuss with patients who are considering genetic testing. One such topic is whether a person would want to know ahead of time whether they have a genetic predisposition for a disease like cancer. A genetic predisposition does not mean that a patient will definitely get a disease, but it can indicate that a person has a higher risk of developing that disease. For some people, the worry and stress of knowing about this risk is too difficult. The counselor helps them think about how the information they receive might affect them and their family. There are no right or wrong opinions or feelings about genetic testing, but it is important to have these discussions in advance. It is the job of the genetic counselor to encourage this discussion.

At the first meeting, the genetic counselor gathers a family health history to help identify which tests to run. Some diseases, such as cancer and Alzheimer's disease, run in families but are not necessarily genetic. Other diseases or conditions that run in families, such as cystic fibrosis and sickle-cell anemia, have been identified as more likely to occur when certain genes or gene mutations are present. A family health history can give genetic counselors a clearer picture of which tests might be most worthwhile.

Genetic counselors sometimes also act as intermediaries between patients and their health insurance providers. Genetic testing can be expensive, so it is important to make sure that the patient's health insurance provider will cover the tests. Negotiating this, in itself, can be a daunting process. Genetic counselors often assist patients with these negotiations.

Once the testing is complete, the genetic counselor reads and interprets the results and then writes a report. The counselor and patient meet once again to discuss the results. This can be emotional for both the counselor who is delivering the results and the patient who is receiving them. Learning about a genetic abnormality or risk can be a big surprise, and some patients are thankful to have this information. Others might feel anxiety, guilt (that they might have passed their condition on to a child), or fear. The genetic counselor explains the findings, what they mean, and how to use the information. Counselors do not tell patients what they should do; rather, they discuss options and listen to their patients' thoughts and concerns. Finally, the counselor follows up with any recommendations or referrals and sometimes meets with other family members.

The story of a thirty-eight-year-old woman named Jackie illustrates the benefits of genetic testing and the journey that patients and genetic counselors take together. Jackie had seen many relatives on her father's side diagnosed with and die from breast or ovarian cancer. Her paternal grandmother died in her forties, and two paternal aunts had also lost their lives to cancer. Jackie's doctor referred her to a genetic counselor after learning about her family history. The genetic counselor helped her decide which tests to do, and eventually she tested positive for a genetic mutation called BRCA1. A person with this mutation has a higher risk of developing breast and ovarian cancer than do those without it. After many discussions, Jackie and her counselor decided on a treatment plan that included increased screenings and preventive surgery. Jackie says she feels empowered by the road map she and her counselor created together, and she is hopeful for a bright future.

Education and Training

Most genetic counselors earn their bachelor's degree in biology or one of the social sciences, such as psychology. After that, a master's degree in genetic counseling takes about two years to complete at one of more than thirty accredited programs in the United States. The master's degree in genetic counseling includes classes in human genetics, birth defects, ethics, counseling, and genetic testing. The master's program also includes hands-on clinical training. In most states, genetic counselors must be certified by the American Board of Genetic Counselors.

Skills and Personality

Genetic counselors need to have strengths in two main areas: intellectual ability and interpersonal skills. This is because the job is equal parts science and social skills. Genetics is a complex science, and test results can be confusing. Counselors must be

Knowledge Is Power

"I guide patients through their decision on whether or not to pursue genetic testing, either during a pregnancy or due to a . . . history of cancer and help them think through the implications of the test results. Genetic counseling brings out the 'human-ness' in all of us—our hopes, our fears, our questions, and our desire for answers. It's a process of bringing the past, present, and future all together in a specific space and time to try and explain . . . history, determine a diagnosis . . . or provide important genetic information for future generations. It's a beautiful process of education, advocacy and empowerment."

—Chelsea Wagner, genetic counselor

Quoted in National Society of Genetic Counselors, "'I Am a Genetic Counselor: A Celebration of Genetic Counselor Awareness Day," *NSGC Blog*, November 14, 2019. www.nsgc.org.

able to clearly communicate what genetic testing can and cannot show and help patients understand their options once test results are available. They must also have empathy. Genetic counselors must be compassionate, sensitive, and able to give support when they have to deliver bad news. "Being a genetic counselor," Julia Platt explains, "means that I can be present in the moments that matter. I sit with my patients when their lives change because of a new life-threatening diagnosis or the new understanding that their relatives may also be predisposed to disease."[21]

Another trait shared by genetic counselors is the desire to be a lifelong learner. Keeping up with the latest research is important. Opportunities to collaborate with other professionals and learn from one another is something that genetic counselors seek out and enjoy about this profession.

Working Conditions

Most genetic counselors work full-time and have regular hours, with little need to work weekends or holidays. They work in comfortable, social environments such as hospitals, clinics, and doctors' offices. Their daily schedules usually include a mix of meetings with patients, analyzing test results, reviewing patient information, and writing reports.

Although most of the time genetic counselors meet with their clients face-to-face, there is a growing trend to offer consultations by telephone. This allows patients who live in rural areas the ability to seek answers to their genetic questions without having to travel far from home.

Employers and Pay

There are a variety of employers to choose from for genetic counselors, with about one-third finding jobs in hospitals. After hospitals, diagnostic and medical labs employ the most genetic counselors. These genetic counselors focus on research, including collecting information such as detailed family histories and pregnancy information, which helps in the development of new or improved treatment or care for people with genetic conditions. Some counselors work in doctors' offices, especially in practices that specialize in cancer and infertility. There are also opportunities at universities teaching others how to become genetic counselors and within public health organizations teaching the public about how genetic testing might be beneficial.

What Is the Future Outlook for Genetic Counselors?

The field of genetic counseling is predicted to grow by at least 27 percent by the year 2028, according to the Bureau of Labor Statistics. This is more than four times more than the average for all careers. Although genetic counseling is a relatively new field, the three thousand genetic counselors working today find that recognition and appreciation for their work is growing. Ongoing scientific discoveries make the job of genetic counselor one that continues to evolve. As Kennedy Burke, a certified genetic counselor shares, "It is an exciting time to be a genetic counselor. The workforce is growing and diversifying, and there is more awareness about the unique value that genetic counselors can bring to the table."[22]

Find Out More

American Society of Human Genetics (ASHG)

www.ashg.org

ASHG is a worldwide group of people who are involved in human genetics. They offer support and information to research scientists, health professionals, and the public. They have a section for students and a section about policies and laws.

Centers for Disease Control and Prevention (CDC)

www.cdc.gov

The CDC website has valuable information about genetic counseling and offers a deeper look at the greater field of genomics and health. It includes sections on family health histories and also about specific genetic diseases and disorders. The "Hot Topics of the Day" section and the "Genomics A–Z" tab both provide a lot of current information.

Genetics Generation

https://knowgenetics.org

This is a great source for anyone looking to learn more about genetics. With basic information, common misconceptions, and case studies to read, there is a lot of information available. The website includes a section about genetic testing and has some interesting links to information about the ethical issues surrounding the topic of genetics.

National Society of Genetic Counselors (NSGC)

www.nsgc.org

The NSGC's interesting website highlights the many facets of genetic counseling. It includes links to educational materials, current news and issues, and resources for patients. Because this field is changing, there is also information about research and public policy.

Respiratory Therapist

What Does a Respiratory Therapist Do?

Respiratory therapists (RTs) are trained to care for people who have a medical condition that makes it hard for them to breathe. They work alongside doctors and nurses. Although many of their patients have chronic (i.e., long-term) conditions, they also encounter situations that require quick thinking and fast action. As one emergency room doctor explains, "If a patient isn't ventilating [breathing] properly, there's nothing we can do to save them."[23]

Respiratory therapists work with patients of all ages. They work with premature infants whose lungs are not fully developed, causing breathing difficulties. They work with elderly people, who are more likely to get diseases that affect the lungs, such as pneumonia. And they work with people of all ages who have chronic conditions that affect their lungs, such as asthma or cystic fibrosis.

Most RTs (about 81 percent) work in hospitals, according to the Bureau of Labor Statistics (BLS). No matter what medical conditions bring people to hospitals, if they are having trouble breathing, they will likely be seen by an RT. This is true whether the problem stems from an emergency or a nonemergency. One type of emergency that would require the presence of an RT is a heart stoppage, or cardiac arrest. If patients arrive at the hospital suffering from cardiac arrest, RTs keep them breathing while doctors work to restart their hearts and stabilize their vital signs. To do this, RTs often use a ventilator, which is a machine that breathes for patients when they cannot breathe on their own.

Stephanie Dirksen has worked as a respiratory therapist for twenty-five years. She recounts one case involving a patient who had come to the emergency room (ER). ER staff had paged Dirksen requesting her immediate assistance. On arriving, Dirksen immediately began a visual assessment of the patient's condition. "He appears to be . . . in respiratory distress," she writes in her description of what she encountered that day. The attending physician ordered another RT to start breathing treatments. At the same time, Dirksen drew blood from the patient and ran it through an analyzer, which measures the levels of oxygen and carbon dioxide in the blood. Too much or not enough of either can be a problem. The test results came quickly: "The patient is in respiratory failure, so I grab a ventilator. . . . The physician announces to prepare for intubation."[24] Intubation is when the RT opens a patient's mouth and inserts a flexible tube down the throat to the lungs. Once Dirksen's patient was intubated, she attached the ventilator and turned it on. Because the patient was now stabilized, she moved on to other patients. But she returned to check the original patient's condition multiple times until the treatment had finished.

Many of the conditions that RTs help treat require long-term treatment. Respiratory therapists educate patients about their medications and how to care for themselves at home. They give patients exercises to help strengthen their lungs. They teach them how to monitor how well their lungs are working to provide oxygen to their body. This education can make a huge difference in the life span and quality of life of patients with lung disease.

The Workday

Respiratory therapists are part of a team. This team—made up of doctors, surgeons, nurses, and other therapists—works together.

However, each person has a specific role to play—and every team member counts. The key to success, says RT Jack Fried, is "dependability, reliability, and credibility—in short, be there when needed."[25]

Patients in the ER are often unconscious and unaware that an RT is present and helping to keep them alive. Because of this, some people call this a thankless job. But as one RT says, "There's nothing thankless . . . about being part of a medical team that saves lives."[26]

There are three stages of interactions between RTs and patients, and the time needed for each stage varies. The first stage involves evaluating the patient through observation, asking questions, and performing basic tests. The arterial blood gas test, which shows how much oxygen and carbon dioxide are in the patient's blood, is commonly used by RTs. Another common test is a pulmonary function test, which requires the patient to breathe into a machine that measures lung capacity. The results show whether the patient needs help breathing or can breathe without assistance. The RT reviews this information with the doctor, who decides whether treatment is needed and, if so, which treatment would be appropriate.

Treatment is the second stage. Therapists have several tools at their disposal, from very basic to high tech. One common emergency treatment is known as "bagging." It involves the patient's mouth and nose being covered by by a breathing mask attached to a bag that is manually squeezed, forcing air into the lungs of a patient who is having trouble breathing. Sometimes RTs have to intubate patients. This allows patients to be connected to a mechanical ventilator, which can breathe for them for a longer time. Some patients find it scary to be intubated and on a breathing machine, so RTs must comfort and calm them.

Monitoring the patient's breathing and oxygen levels and adjusting the treatment plan, if needed, is the last stage. When the patient is stable, or no longer needs help breathing, the RT can move on to other patients.

Education and Training

An RT is a highly trained professional. Respiratory therapist John Inkrott wants people to know that RTs "do more than give breathing treatments"[27] and are a specialized part of a medical team. Becoming an RT requires a high school diploma and a two-year associate's degree. The second year of the program is spent getting hands-on experience in clinics. There are at least four hundred accredited RT programs in the United States. Taking classes in anatomy, chemistry, and math in high school is a great way to prepare for this career.

After they finish their degree, all RTs must pass a certification test. Most states also require a license to practice. There is a growing trend to also obtain a bachelor's degree, but this is not a requirement. For many people, going to school for two years after high school and ending up with a respected, well-paying job is very appealing. Respiratory therapist Cindy Goff says she is "thankful to be an RT because this profession has provided me and my family with a wonderful livelihood."[28]

Respiratory therapists must stay up-to-date on the latest equipment, devices, and treatments. This often requires completing additional classes or training throughout their career.

Skills and Personality

Like other health professionals who provide patient care, RTs have to be good listeners and clear communicators. They have

Self-Care Matters

"Take care of yourself! Respiratory therapy is an intense profession that affects the life and death of your patient. The profession can take a toll if you do not make it a point to relieve stress and put your health first. Also, treat every patient like they are one of your loved ones. Being a patient can be scary. It is important to connect with your patients and to comfort them."

—Jen Spurlin, respiratory therapist

Quoted in Pima Medical Institute, "The Places You Can Go as a Respiratory Therapist," *PMI Blog,* March 1, 2019. https://pmi.edu.

to be responsive and able to carry out directions from doctors. Some RTs say this makes the job less stressful because they do not have sole responsibility for a patient's welfare. Good communication with the rest of the medical team is key. Respiratory therapist Charlene Barnes explains that she and her colleagues "make recommendations, call the physician, stay proactive in the course of treatment of the patient."[29]

Many careers in health care attract people who want to help others. Compassion and kindness are key traits for good RTs. They see people in crisis and people who have difficult, long-term medical conditions. The ability to empathize and connect with these patients is important. Being a good problem solver and paying attention to detail are also valuable skills. A patient's breathing can change quickly, so RTs must be alert and act fast to respond to a patient's changing medical needs. The hospital environment can be tense, so being able to deal with stress and remain calm under pressure is also critical.

Working Conditions

This is a fast-paced job, and no two days are ever the same. Experienced RTs say that each season brings different respira-

Code Blue

"It's your patient. If you see something is wrong . . . if you suspect things aren't right . . . and a notion in the back of your mind says, 'call for help!' [then] go for it! You only get one chance at this life. I have seen such actions many times save a life. . . . Don't feel stupid! Don't feel bad because you called the team and their services weren't needed. We have all been there. . . .

There is an old saying that goes well here. 'You do the best with what you know today, and as you learn more you do better.'"

—John Bottrell, respiratory therapist

John Bottrell, "Don't Hesitate to Call a Code," *Respiratory Therapy Cave* (blog), November 4, 2019. http://respiratorytherapycave.blogspot.com.

tory emergencies to the ER. In the fall, they treat more cases of asthma, and winter is the viral respiratory illness season. In the summer, they treat more patients for injuries and trauma.

Respiratory therapists who work in hospitals often work long shifts that might include nights and weekends. On busy days, RTs may work many hours without a break. They need to be physically fit because they can be on their feet for hours at a time and may have to help lift or move patients.

Employers and Pay

Hospitals are by far the biggest employers of RTs, but about 15 percent work in home health care, outpatient settings, or long-term care facilities, according to the BLS. An even smaller percentage work in education, training the RTs of the future.

The BLS reports that the average salary in 2018 was between $59,900 and $61,3170, with the highest salaries found on the East and West Coasts. California; Washington, DC; Alaska; and New York are the places where RTs earn an average of $75,000 a year, according to the BLS.

What Is the Future Outlook for Respiratory Therapists?

The BLS projects at least a 21 percent job growth in the respiratory therapy field through 2028. This is much higher than the outlook for job growth overall, and it is also very high for a career that only requires an associate's degree.

Many factors contribute to the demand for more RTs. The Centers for Disease Control and Prevention estimates that 15 million adults live with chronic obstructive pulmonary disease (COPD). COPD is a long-term inflammatory lung disease that results in reduced lung function. In addition, air pollution contributes to lung issues. And an aging population is more susceptible to respiratory illnesses. For these and other reasons, RTs have job security and a well-paid career without the need for extensive schooling, a career path that is appealing to many young people today.

Find Out More

American Association for Respiratory Care (AARC)
www.aarc.org

The AARC website offers information for both its members and the general public. It provides online courses, links to many online resources and articles, and career opportunities. It also has a section for students who are studying to become RTs.

Healthline
www.healthline.com

In the article "What Is a Respiratory Therapist?," Healthline provides general information about the career, including the different types of RTs and their backgrounds and training. It also has information about diseases like COPD and other health information and articles.

National Board for Respiratory Care (NBRC)
www.nbrc.org

The NBRC works to promote excellence in respiratory care. Its website includes a section with information for prospective RTs, certified practitioners, and educators. It also promotes a campaign called "Choose One: Every Breath Counts" to promote better respiratory health.

Respiratory Therapy Zone
www.respiratorytherapyzone.com

Aimed at current and future students, this website offers clear, easy-to-understand information. It provides interesting answers to commonly asked questions such as "What is the difference between an RT and an RN?" There are articles and blog posts as well.

Radiologist

What Does a Radiologist Do?

When a person has a broken bone, he or she usually undergoes an X-ray. When a person shows signs of a tumor, the doctor might order a magnetic resonance imaging (MRI) scan. X-rays and MRIs are two commonly used types of medical imaging (or radiology). The specialist who reviews and evaluates these and other forms of medical imaging is called a radiologist. Radiologists are medical doctors who are trained in the use of various medical imaging procedures for diagnosis and treatment of illnesses and injuries.

The images generated by these scans allow doctors to look inside the human body without surgery, or with minimally invasive procedures. Radiologists read and interpret the results. The reports they generate can be used to help identify an injury or illness—or rule it out. Their evaluations can also be used to help determine appropriate treatment. "Most if not all patients interact with radiology in one way or another, either in the process of disease screening, intervention, diagnosis . . . [or] follow up,"[30] explains Dr. Rachita Khot, a radiologist who works and teaches at the University of Virginia School of Medicine.

A Few Facts

Number of Jobs
37,200 in 2018

Pay
Average salary of
$350,000 in 2018

Educational Requirements
Doctor of medicine or doctor of osteopathic medicine degree

Personal Qualities
Analytical, decisive, collaborative, confident

Work Settings
Hospitals, outpatient clinics, specialty medical centers

Future Job Outlook
10 percent increase by 2028

Radiologists use many types of medical imaging procedures. X-rays use radiation to produce images of the body's internal structures. X-rays are typically used to look for bone problems or issues, such as degeneration, fractures or dislocations, or bone diseases. Also common are MRIs, which use magnets and radio waves to generate detailed images of the structures inside the body. The images are viewed as cross sections, or slices, of the part of the body being viewed. They are often used to look for internal injuries and tumors. These images also allow doctors to "see" inside the brain and spinal cord.

Radiologists rarely meet directly with patients. They work most often with other doctors. Their role is primarily to interpret imaging results and report their findings to the patients' doctors. The bulk of the radiologist's day is spent studying images and writing reports or conferring with other doctors.

Some radiologists are generalists, meaning they perform a wide variety of tests on every part of the human body. Others have a specialty. Interventional radiology is one specialty that is in high demand. Interventional radiologists (IRs) treat diseases and perform minimally invasive procedures using images (MRI, X-ray, ultrasound) to guide them. IRs can use less invasive techniques, such as injections, to precisely target treatments for a number of medical conditions. Radiologists in this specialty have more contact with patients than most other radiologists. This is because they are not just reading images but actually using them to perform noninvasive medical procedures such as biopsies, draining fluids, guiding injections, and shrinking tumors. They also work in hospital operating rooms with teams of nurses and doctors. During surgery, IRs make small incisions and guide a catheter (a flexible tube) with a camera to the area they want to observe in the patient's body. This camera is so small that it can travel through blood vessels. The camera sends images to a screen, which shows the doctors what is going on inside the patient. They may also snip out some tissue to study. In this way, IRs can help diagnose heart disease, stroke, cancer, and many other conditions.

The Best Job in Medicine

"I love radiology because it is the perfect intersection of the art and science of medicine. Expert knowledge of anatomy, pathology, physiology, physics and clinical medicine must be integrated. Every patient is unique. We use the most sophisticated technology in the world to look inside the human body to help solve problems. We see a variety of different diseases in both adults and children, and we play an integral role in the clinical care team. Modern radiology covers all aspects of medicine and there is a great mix of diagnosis and intervention."

—Kristin DeStigter, diagnostic radiologist

Quoted in Jennifer Nachbur, "3 Questions with Chair of Radiology Kristen DeStigter, M.D.," Larner College of Medicine, University of Vermont, September 29, 2017. www.med.uvm.edu.

Other radiology specialties include oncologic (cancer) radiology and cardiac (heart) radiology.

Radiologists usually work behind the scenes. In a hospital emergency room (ER), patients are often unconscious when they arrive and are unable to give medical staff any information about why they are there. Doctors in the ER rely on radiologists to help them determine the problem, especially if there is no visible injury. In this way, MRIs, X-rays, and ultrasounds allow the radiologist to look inside a patient's body without cutting it open. The information gained from imaging is invaluable to other doctors. Dr. Jack Sava, the director of trauma at MedStar Washington Hospital Center puts it this way, "You can't really deliver top-level trauma care without a great . . . team. The collaboration between surgeons and . . . radiologists has been at the center of many great advancements in trauma care"[31] The radiologist's ability to look inside the body without surgery can be a critical part of saving lives in the ER.

The Workday

Although radiologists are all trained to do the same diagnostic tests, their daily routine varies greatly by specialty and where they work. Most radiologists consult with doctors who refer patients

Radiologists read and interpret patient X-rays and MRI scans. Their evaluations can be used to help determine appropriate treatment for patients.

for testing. In this sense, their workday differs from that of most other doctors, who have appointments with patients. Radiologists do not examine patients or take their medical history; rather, they go by the referring doctor's notes. For example, a diagnostic radiologist might work in a breast care center that performs mammograms. The patient's primary care doctor refers the patient, and the same doctor also discusses the results of the mammogram with the patient. The radiologist is not in the room where the mammogram happens; instead, a radiology tech is responsible for positioning the patient and operating the machinery. These images are sent to the radiologist, who reads and interprets them. But even though radiologists do not meet patients, they are critical to their health.

One woman in North Carolina had breast cancer at the age of forty-six, which was treated successfully. Afterward, she had yearly mammograms. A few years later, there were signs that the cancer had returned. She was sent for an in-depth diagnostic mammogram and an MRI so that a radiologist could get a better look. Tests like these help doctors tell the difference between cancer and scar tissue from previous treatments. The patient shares, "I was really happy about this option because it was not invasive— no needles or scarring. I was also reassured by the doctors . . . that they would find out what was going on with me."[32]

Education and Training

Becoming a radiologist takes at least twelve years after high school, requiring dedication and hard work. First, a four-year college degree is earned, followed by four years of medical school. All doctors must do a residency to become a radiologist, and this takes another four years. During residency, doctors focus on radiation safety, technology, minimally invasive procedures, and how to interpret all types of imaging exams. Doctors also undergo extensive training on all of the different imaging machines they will use.

Like all medical doctors, radiologists must pass licensing and board certification exams. Once they cross this threshold, they can begin practicing medicine. However, many choose to pursue a fellowship to specialize in a specific area, such as breast or brain imaging, which can take an additional one to two years.

Skills and Personality

Radiologists must have excellent technical and analytical skills. They work with a lot of sophisticated machinery and collect and interpret complex, technical data. They also must be confident in their abilities because they have to make decisions and recommendations with authority.

During medical school, some students are drawn to radiology because it differs from other specialties in terms of personal strengths and work environment. Radiologists work with other doctors, so they must have strong collaboration and communication skills, both in writing and in person. They need to be organized and self-motivated because they have a busy schedule and a lot of paperwork to manage. Often, they are in charge of a team of technicians and assistants, so management skills are an asset. But since they do not interact with patients face-to-face, it is a specialty that appeals to people who might prefer this. Finally, many radiologists work in hospitals where speed and accuracy are of the utmost importance. They must perform well under pressure and be able to quickly make decisions.

Working Conditions

Radiologists who work in hospitals rarely have set, regular hours and are often on call. In fact, many hospitals require that their medical staff, including radiologists, live within a certain proximity to the hospital so they can get there quickly. Many radiology practices that serve hospitals have a rotating schedule to cover night and weekend shifts. Teleradiology is a newer concept, where the doctor can consult by telephone and computer. This can reduce the need for night coverage and also help people living in rural areas.

Employers and Pay

Radiologists are both highly respected and highly paid, with an average salary of $350,000 per year. The states with the highest paid radiologists in 2018, according to the Bureau of Labor Statistics (BLS) were Maryland, Connecticut, Washington, and Illinois. Radiologists in these states average well over $425,000 each year.

Radiologists typically work in one of three settings: hospitals, outpatient clinics, and freestanding specialty medical centers. In a hospital, they often work with the ER, using their skills to help diagnose patients who come in with an emergency. In a specialty medical center they specialize in an area that uses imaging to diagnose and treat patients, such as breast care or cancer care. Other specialty medical centers focus on sports medicine or treatment for vein disorders.

In the ER, the IRs Save Lives

"The patients have the vast majority of their life ahead of them. We do a huge service for these patients and watching them leave the hospital is immensely gratifying. The gratification of saving a life, of doing a procedure and immediately seeing the impact on the patient, makes all of those late-night calls worthwhile."

—Darryl Zuckerman, radiologist

Quoted in Susan Rose, "IR in the ER: The Key Role IR Plays on the Trauma Team," *IRQuarterly*, Fall 2017. https://connect.sirweb.org.

What Is the Future Outlook for Radiologists?

The field of radiology is predicted to grow by at least 10 percent by 2028, according to the BLS. Radiology is one of the most technologically advanced fields in medicine, and new technology is always being developed. A trend toward less invasive procedures for diagnosis and treatment of cancer and other diseases is also pushing the increased demand for qualified radiologists. As Dr. Khot explains, "The explosion in knowledge and technology in modern medicine has completely transformed the concept of clinical diagnosis and treatment . . . These changes along with the advent of modern imaging tools have made [radiology and medical imaging] the definitive diagnostic tool for many diseases, as well as . . . [for] monitoring treatment and predicting outcomes."[33]

Find Out More

American Board of Radiology (ABR)

www.theabr.org

The ABR helps patients and supports physicians. Its website has sections specific to diagnostic and interventional specialties as well as radiation oncology. It also includes a news section with industry-specific articles.

American College of Radiology (ACR)
www.acr.org

This ACR website offers a wide variety of information about radiology for both patients and professionals. It includes a section on current research and also one that breaks down and clearly explains the various subspecialties.

RadiologyEd.org
https://radiologyed.org

This is a great place to research career opportunities in radiology. There is information about how to become a radiology or cardiovascular technologist, a radiologist assistant, an MRI or ultrasound technician, and other related careers. It also includes sections about school options and degrees, employment opportunities, and salaries.

RadiologyInfo.org
www.radiologyinfo.org

This easy-to-understand site discusses over two hundred radiological procedures. It includes sections that explain the tests and treatments available, the related diseases and conditions, and pediatric treatments, among others.

Source Notes

New Frontiers in Medicine
1. Jalila Cunningham, "Into the Night," *The Hospitalist,* July 2011. www.the-hospitalist.org.

Medical Scientist
2. Quoted in Inside Career Info, "Inside Medical Scientist Careers: Things You Need to Know, but Nobody Tells You." www.insidecareerinfo.com.
3. Quoted in Inside Career Info, "Inside Medical Scientist Careers."
4. Quoted in Alison White, "What the Experts Said: Routes into Medical Research Careers," *The Guardian* (Manchester, UK), March 14, 2011. www.theguardian.com.

Physician Assistant
5. Quoted in Megan Anderson, "Interview with a Physician Assistant Working in the ER," Health eCareers, June 5, 2019. www.healthecareers.com.
6. Quoted in Anderson, "Interview with a Physician Assistant Working in the ER."
7. Quoted in Anderson, "Interview with a Physician Assistant Working in the ER."
8. Quoted in *U.S. News & World Report*, "Best Healthcare Jobs: Physician Assistant." https://money.usnews.com.

Prosthetist
9. Quoted in P.K. Daniel, "From Amputee to Clinical Prosthetist: Four Journeys," *Lower Extremity Review,* October 2015. https://lermagazine.com.
10. Quoted in *U.S. News & World Report,* "Best Healthcare Support Jobs: Orthotist and Prosthetist." https://money.usnews .com.

11. Quoted in *U.S. News & World Report,* "Best Healthcare Support Jobs: Orthotist and Prosthetist."

Nurse Anesthetist

12. Quoted in Assessment Technologies Institute, "Inside Look: The Day-to-Day of a Nurse Anesthetist," *ATI Nursing Education* (blog), October 12, 2017. https://atinursingblog.com.
13. Quoted in Assessment Technologies Institute, "Inside Look."
14. Quoted in Robin Farmer, "Why You Should Consider Becoming a Nurse Anesthetist," Daily Nurse: The Pulse of Nursing, June 14, 2016. https://dailynurse.com.
15. Quoted in *U.S. News & World Report,* "Best Paying Jobs: Nurse Anesthetist." https://money.usnews.com.

Medical Services Manager

16. Quoted in *U.S. News & World Report,* "Best Business Jobs: Medical Health Services Manager." https://money.usnews.com.
17. Quoted in UW HIMT Team, "Health Information Manager Shares the Joys and Challenges of Leading UW Health's HIM Department," Health Information Management & Technology, University of Wisconsin, July 23, 2015. https://himt.wisconsin.edu.
18. Quoted in Nina Chamlou, "Protecting Patient Data—an Interview with AHIMA's Cheryl Martin," Medical Technology Schools. www.medicaltechnologyschools.com.
19. Quoted in *U.S. News & World Report,* "Best Business Jobs."

Genetic Counselor

20. Quoted in *U.S. News & World Report,* "Best Healthcare Support Jobs: Genetic Counselor." https://money.usnews.com.
21. Quoted in National Society of Genetic Counselors, "'I am a Genetic Counselor': A Celebration of Genetic Counselor Awareness Day," *NSGC Blog,* November 14, 2019. www.nsgc.org.
22. Quoted in National Society of Genetic Counselors, "'I am a Genetic Counselor.'"

Respiratory Therapist

23. Quoted in Stephanie Dirksen, "A Day in the Life of a Respiratory Therapist," Clinician Today, August 29, 2018. https://cliniciantoday.com.
24. Dirksen, "A Day in the Life of a Respiratory Therapist."
25. American Association for Respiratory Care, "R-E-S-P-E-C-T: Earning It in Respiratory Therapy." www.aarc.org.
26. Dirksen, "A Day in the Life of a Respiratory Therapist."
27. Quoted in American Association for Respiratory Care, "R-E-S-P-E-C-T."
28. Quoted in American Association for Respiratory Care, "Why I'm Thankful to Be a Respiratory Therapist." www.aarc.org.
29. Quoted in American Association for Respiratory Care, "R-E-S-P-E-C-T."

Radiologist

30. Quoted in University of Virginia School of Medicine, "What Is a Radiologist?," July 11, 2017. https://med.virginia.edu.
31. Quoted in Susan Rose, "IR in the ER: The Key Role IR Plays on the Trauma Team," IRQuarterly, Fall 2017. https://connect.sirweb.org.
32. Quoted in Wake Radiology, "A Breast MRI at Wake Radiology Discovered the Truth," December 13, 2012. www.wakerad.com.
33. Quoted in University of Virginia School of Medicine, "What Is a Radiologist?"

Interview with a Genetic Counselor

Audrey Brown is a genetic counselor at the University of Colorado Cancer Center. She has worked as a genetic counselor for almost two years. She answered questions about her career by email.

Q: Why did you become a genetic counselor?
A: Genetic counseling, for me, is a perfect career to balance my love for science and helping others. I always knew I wanted to work in health care. I really enjoy being able to help others understand complex science and data in a way that is useful to them and can make a difference in their health. Medical school sounded too long, pharmacy school required too much chemistry, and nursing sounded appealing—but let's be honest, I don't have the stomach to handle that. Once I learned about genetic counseling, it seemed like the perfect fit! In addition, genetics hits close to home because my older sister has a genetic condition called neurofibromatosis type 1. She has a mild form of the disease, but because of her diagnosis, genetics was always a subtle part of my life. Once I was old enough to better understand her genetic condition and how it impacted her, I found it so interesting and decided I wanted to learn more and continue helping others understand more about themselves.

Q: Where did you go to school and what degree(s) did you need to become a genetic counselor?
A: I got my undergraduate degree in biology at a small school in Iowa called Wartburg College. I then went on to graduate school at the University of Colorado to get my master's in genetic counseling.

It is important to make sure when applying to genetic counseling graduate school programs that you have taken all of the prerequisite classes. Each program requires slightly different coursework.

Q: Can you describe your workday?

A: One fantastic thing about genetic counseling is that there are so many different career opportunities within the field that you can find a work setting that best suits you. Genetic counselors work in hospitals and private centers, from home doing telephone counseling, in laboratories, at the public health department, and many more locations. Genetic counselors can specialize in prenatal [genetic testing], pediatrics, cardiology, neurology, lab work, cancer, and the list goes on. We act as educators, patient advocates, providers, resource centers, etc.

I currently work in a hereditary cancer center at an academic institution. Here, I get the opportunity to see patients; order genetic testing; call out, interpret, and explain genetic test results; write follow-up letters; and discuss cancer screening and risks. I also get to be part of training graduate students, giving lectures, and educating other providers and people in the community about hereditary cancer genetic testing.

Q: What do you like the most about your job?

A: I am such a people person that I truly love being able to meet with patients and build relationships with them. Sometimes I will have the opportunity to meet with an entire family throughout the genetic testing process, and it is so fun to get to know them. In addition, it is a rewarding career knowing I am helping others on a daily basis!

Q: What do you like the least about your job?

A: Sometimes, even if a family has a really strong family history of cancer and certainly looks like there should be a hereditary explanation, genetic testing is negative. This is frustrating for patients because they just want to understand why there is so much cancer in the family. In turn, this is frustrating for me as well because I feel at a loss that I am unable to make sense of what is going on, and I wish I could always provide answers.

Q: What personal qualities do you find most valuable for this type of work?

A: Genetic counseling is definitely made for individuals who love to learn and will continue to love to learn throughout their entire career. Genetics is a rapidly growing field, so staying up to date on the most recent advances in all of the different areas of genetics is no small task. In addition, genetic counselors tend to be compassionate and often have to act as advocates for their patients to make sure they have all the right resources they need.

Q: Can you describe a memorable moment or client that stands out, and why?

A: I have a few clients and moments that have become memorable to me in my career, but what stands out the most to me is when patients thank me and then trust me enough to recommend their family members come to me as well. As a genetic counselor, I sometimes see patients in very vulnerable positions that can be uncomfortable for them, so when they thank me, and trust me enough to also see their siblings, children, etc., it makes me feel really good.

Q: What advice do you have for students who might be interested in this career?

A: Experience. Experience. Experience. It is important when applying to genetic counseling programs that you are sure this is the career you want to pursue. Programs are small and competitive, so having a lot of different types of experiences that can be applicable to genetic counseling is not only helpful to help you decide if this is what you want to do, but it also looks great on applications for school. Experience can come through shadowing genetic counselors in your area, volunteering at crisis hotlines/domestic violence shelters, volunteering for your local Special Olympics, etc. I would also recommend taking biology/genetics courses as electives if those are options available to you.

Other Jobs in Medicine

Addiction/substance abuse counselor
Athletic trainer
Audiologist
Biomedical engineer
Cancer immunologist
Cardiovascular technologist
Clinical informatics specialist
Dentist
Dietitian/nutritionist
Family nurse practitioner
Gerontologist
Health care navigator
Home health aide
Lifestyle medicine physician
Marriage and family therapist
Medical assistant
Medical scribe
Medical virtualist (telemedicine)
Nurse-midwife
Occupational therapist
Pediatrician
Pharmacy technician
Phlebotomist
Physical therapy assistant
Public health educator
Radiation therapist
Registered nurse
Robotic assistance nurse
Sonographer
Speech-language pathologist
Three-dimensional printer

Editor's note: The online *Occupational Outlook Handbook* of the US Department of Labor's Bureau of Labor Statistics is an excellent source of information on jobs in hundreds of career fields, including many of those listed here. The *Occupational Outlook Handbook* may be accessed online at www.bls.gov/ooh.

Index

Picture Credits